JELLY BELLY

Text copyright © 1983 Dennis Lee
Illustrations copyright © 1983 Juan Wijngaard
Design: Robert B McNab

First published 1983 by Blackie and Son Ltd.
Furnival House
14/18 High Holborn
London WC1V 6BX

Published in the United States of America by
Peter Bedrick Books
125 East 23 Street
New York NY 10010

Library of Congress Catalog Card Number 84-45915

ISBN 0 87226 001 1

Printed in Great Britain by
Blantyre Printing & Binding Ltd.,
London and Glasgow

JELLY BELLY

Dennis Lee

Illustrated by Juan Wijngaard

Bedrick/Blackie

Contents

Title	Page
The Dreadful Doings of Jelly Belly	6
Lazy Liza Briggs	8
Little Miss Dimble	9
Hugh, Hugh	10
Mrs Magee	12
There Was An Old Lady	14
Kitty-cat, Kitty-cat	16
The Garbage Men	17
Easy, Peasy	17
Bundle-buggy Boogie	18
No	20
Dickery Dean	20
Dawdle, Dawdle, Dawdle	21

Fingers and Toes
(Action Rhymes)

Three Tickles	22
Doodle-y-doo	22
Counting Out	22
The Army Went A-marching	23
Boogie Tricks	24
Chicoutimi Town	24
The Kitty Ran Up the Tree	25
Five Fat Fleas	26
The Seven Kinds of Bees	27

The Puzzle	28
Can You Canoe?	29
Freddy	29
Skit, Scat	30
Catching	30
Meet Me	30
Spaghetti-o!	31
Eh, Mon	31
Double-barrelled Ding-dong-bat	31
Dirty Georgie	32
News of the Day	33

Jenny Shall Ride	33
The Maple Tree	34
Shoo, Doggie, Shoo!	34
Mr Lister's Dog	34
Carey Cut	35
Over and Over	36
Under the Garden Hose	36
Knock! Knock!	37
Doctor, Doctor	37
Sailing to Sea	38
The Voyage	39
Rock Me Easy	40
The Little Old Man	41
The Bear and the Bees	42
The Tiny Perfect Mayor	42
Bigamy Bill	43
Dopey the Dinosaur	43
The Dinosaur Dinner	44
Torontosaurus Rex	44
Anna Banana	45
Peter Stampeder	46
Robber J Badguy	46
William Lyon Mackenzie	47
Peterkin Pete	47
The Excellent Wedding of the Broom and the Mop	48
Mrs Murphy, and Mrs Murphy's Kids	50
My Doodle-bug Won't Come Home	52
Pussy-willow	53
Granny Spider	53
The Queen of Sheba's Daughter	54
Little Mr Mousiekin	54
Zinga, Zinga	55
The Ghost and Jenny Jemima	56
The Birthday Present	58
Thumbelina	59
Up in North Ontario	60
Christmas Tree	60
Going, Going, Gone	61
The Snowstorm	61
The Gentle Giant	62
Good Night, Good Night	63
Silverly	64

The Dreadful Doings of Jelly Belly

Jelly Belly bit
    With a big fat bite.
Jelly Belly fought
    With a big fat fight.

Jelly Belly scowled
    With a big fat frown.
Jelly Belly yelled
    Till his house fell down.

Liza Briggs

Lazy lousy Liza Briggs
Wouldn't get up to feed the pigs.
The pigs pulled off the comforter
And jumped right into bed with her.

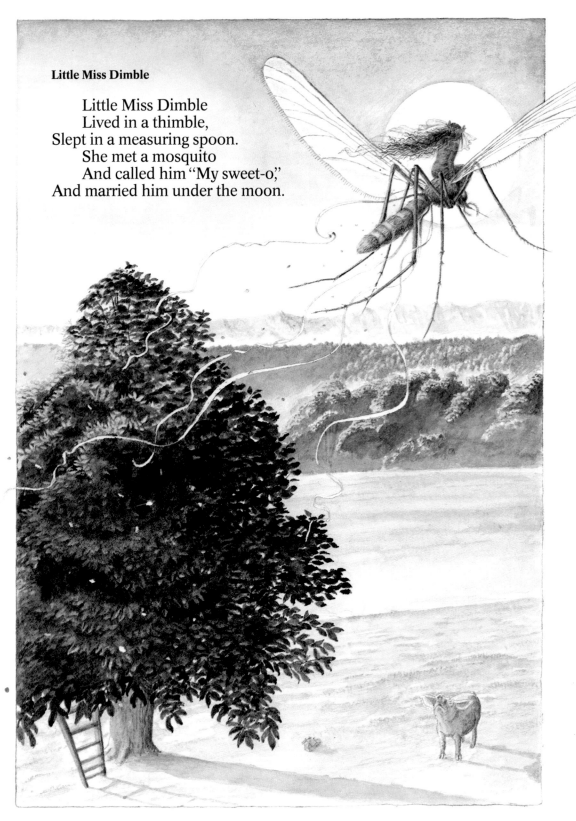

Little Miss Dimble

Little Miss Dimble
Lived in a thimble,
Slept in a measuring spoon.
She met a mosquito
And called him "My sweet-o,"
And married him under the moon.

Hugh, Hugh

Hugh, Hugh,
At the age of two,
Built his house in a big brown shoe.
Hugh, Hugh,
What'll you do?
There's holes in the soles
And the rain comes through!

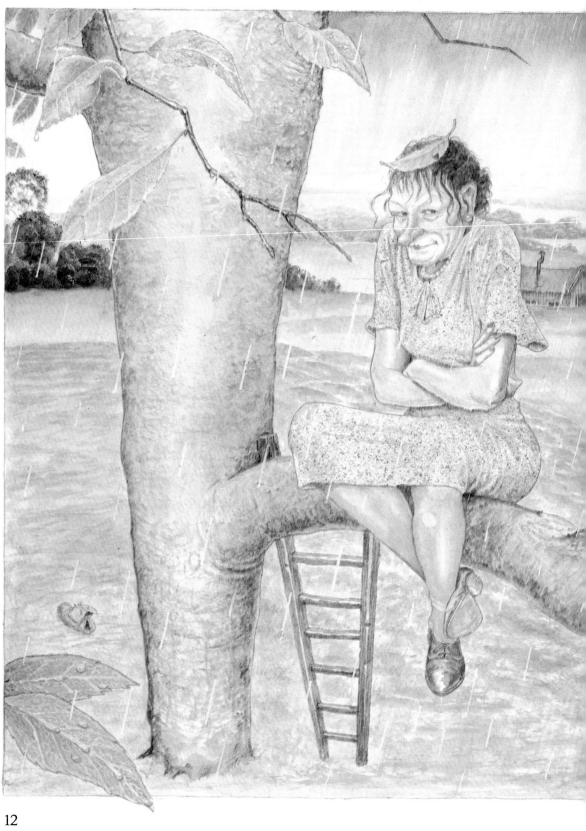

Mrs Magee

Mrs Magee
Climbed into a tree,
And she only came down to go shopping.
A branch was her bed,
With a leaf on her head—
And whenever it rained, she got sopping.

13

There Was An Old Lady

There was an old lady
    Whose kitchen was bare,
So she called for the cat
    Saying, "Time for some air!"

She sent him to buy her
    A packet of cheese.
But the cat hurried back
    With a basket of bees.

She sent him to buy her
    A gallon of juice.
But the cat reappeared
    With a galloping goose.

She sent him to buy her
    A dinner of beef.
But the cat scampered home
    With an Indian chief.

She sent him to buy her
    A bowl of ice cream.
But the cat skated in
    With a whole hockey team.

She sent him to buy her
    A bite of spaghetti.
But the cat strutted up
    With a bride and confetti.

She sent him to buy her
    A fine cup of tea.
But the cat waddled back
    With a dinosaur's knee.

The fridge was soon bulging,
    And so was the shelf.
So she sent for a hot dog
    And ate it herself.

Kitty-cat, Kitty-cat

Kitty-cat,
Kitty-cat,
Will you be mine?
I'll bring you
Milk and I'll
Make your coat shine.

You'll be my
Puss, and you'll
Sleep in my bed—
Under the
Coverlet,
Right by my head.

The Garbage Men

What a lucky
    Bit of luck—
The garbage men
    In the garbage truck!

One has a can, and
    One has a pan, and
One is a big fat
    Canadian!

Easy, Peasy

Easy, peasy, paperboy,
Patch your coat with corduroy,
Marching like a soldier boy,
    Bringing us the paper.

Bundle-buggy Boogie

Well, way up north
On a fine bright day,
A bundle-buggy boogied
At the break of day.

It did the boogie-woogie here,
It did the boogie-woogie there,
It did the bundle-buggy boogie-woogie
Ev-er-y-where:

    Calabogie,
    Kapuskasing,
    Espanola,
    Atikokan;
    Manitoulin,
    Madawaska,
    Mindemoya,
    Moosonee!

Then another bundle-buggy
Did a boogie-woogie hop,
And another and another
In the bundle-boogie bop.

And it's boogie-woogie high,
And it's boogie-woogie low,
And it's bundle-buggy boogie-woogie
Everywhere you go:

    Athabasca,
    Abitibi,
    Bona Vista,
    Malaspina;
    Bella Bella,
    Bella Coola,
    Batchawana,
    Baie Comeau!

No

No, no, no!
They're always saying no.
Is nothing ever good enough
But no, no, no?

Dickery Dean

"What's the matter
    With Dickery Dean?
He jumped right into
    The washing machine!"

"Nothing's the matter
    With Dickery Dean—
He dove in dirty,
    And he jumped out clean!"

Dawdle, Dawdle, Dawdle

Dawdle, dawdle, dawdle,
It's the uncles and the aunts,
Dawdling with their shoes and socks,
Dawdling with their pants.
    So hurry up
    And scurry up
    And hurry, scurry, worry up—
Thank goodness there are kids around
To make them stop their dawdling.

Dawdle, dawdle, dawdle,
It's the daddies and the mums,
Dawdling with their apple-juice,
Dawdling with their crumbs.
    So hurry up
    And scurry up
    And hurry, scurry, worry up—
Thank *goodness* there are kids around
To make them stop their dawdling!

Three Tickles

Pizza, pickle,
Pumpernickel,
My little guy
Shall have a tickle:

One for his nose,
And one for his toes,
And one for his tummy
Where the hot dog goes.

Doodle-y-doo

Doodle-y-doo,
Doodle-y-doo:
I lost my baby,
And what shall I do?

Doodle-y-dee,
Doodle-y-dee:
Open my fingers
And what do I see?

A baby!

Counting Out

One for coffee
One for tea
And one to run
To Calgary.

22

The Army Went A-marching

Oh the army went a-marching
    And they marched across the tum;
Round and round the tummy with a
    Mighty army drum.

And it's first toe,
    Second toe,
    Third toe, and
    Four;
Tickle the top of the fifth toe—
    And then you march some more.

Oh the army went a-hopping
    And they hopped across the snout;
Round and round the sneezer with a
    Mighty army shout.

And it's first toe,
    Second toe,
    Third toe, and
    Four;
Tickle the tip of the fifth toe—
    And then you hop some more.

Boogie Tricks

One, two, three:
The cat ran up the tree.

Four, five, six:
He did some boogie tricks.

Seven, eight, nine:
He boogied on the line.

Ten, eleven, twelve:
He boogied by himself.

Chicoutimi Town

Which is the way to Chicoutimi town?
Left foot up, and right foot down.
Right foot up and left foot down,
That is the way to Chicoutimi town.

The Kitty Ran Up the Tree

The kitty ran up the tree,
The kitty ran up the tree,
    Her nose went up
    And her toes went up
And the kitty ran up the tree.

Why did she climb the tree?
To see what a kitty could see.
    But all she could see
    At the top of the tree
Was the tip of the top of the tree—

      So—

The kitty came down the tree,
The kitty came down the tree,
    Her nose came down
    And her toes came down
And the kitty came down the tree.

Five Fat Fleas

Five fat fleas
Upon a trapeze
Did somersaults one by one.
A flea flew, a flea flew,
A flea flew, a flea flew,
A flea flew, and then there were none.

Four fat frogs
On tumbledown logs
Did somersaults one by one.
A frog flew, a frog flew,
A frog flew, a frog flew,
(Clap), and then there were none.

Three fat cats
On calico mats
Did somersaults one by one.
A cat flew, a cat flew,
A cat flew, *(clap)*,
(Clap), and then there were none.

Two fat ants
In dancing pants
Did somersaults one by one.
An ant flew, an ant flew,
(Clap), *(clap)*,
(Clap), and then there were none.

One fat bee
On a billygoat's knee
Did somersaults one by one.
A bee flew, *(clap)*,
(Clap), *(clap)*,
(Clap), and then there were none.

No fat gnomes
On a dinosaur's bones
Did somersaults none by none.
    (Clap), (clap),
    (Clap), (clap),
(Clap), and then there were none.

One fat bee
On a billygoat's knee
Did somersaults one by one.
    A bee flew, *(clap),*
    (Clap), (clap),
(Clap), and then there were none.

    Two fat ants
    (Etcetera, ad nauseam).

The Seven Kinds of Bees

Now, there are seven kinds of bees:
Bees that buzz, and bees that tease,
Bees that tickle, bees with fleas,
And bees with burrs upon their knees,
Bees that shyly murmur Please—
And bees that nip your nose off!

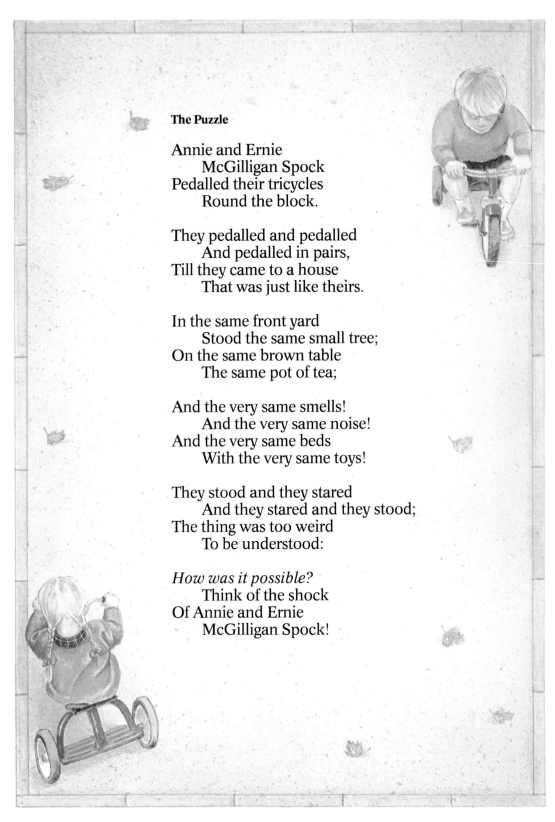

The Puzzle

Annie and Ernie
    McGilligan Spock
Pedalled their tricycles
    Round the block.

They pedalled and pedalled
    And pedalled in pairs,
Till they came to a house
    That was just like theirs.

In the same front yard
    Stood the same small tree;
On the same brown table
    The same pot of tea;

And the very same smells!
    And the very same noise!
And the very same beds
    With the very same toys!

They stood and they stared
    And they stared and they stood;
The thing was too weird
    To be understood:

How was it possible?
    Think of the shock
Of Annie and Ernie
    McGilligan Spock!

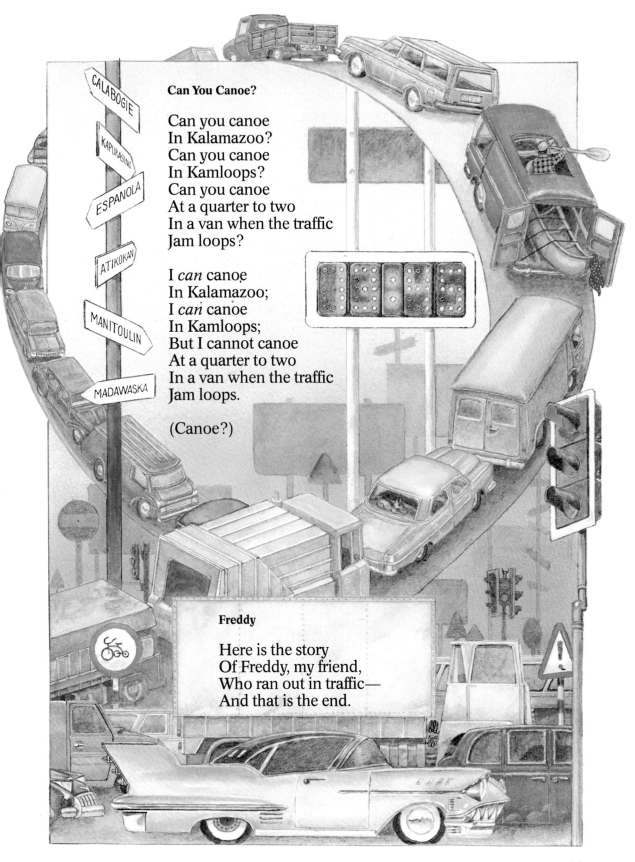

Can You Canoe?

Can you canoe
In Kalamazoo?
Can you canoe
In Kamloops?
Can you canoe
At a quarter to two
In a van when the traffic
Jam loops?

I *can* canoe
In Kalamazoo;
I *can* canoe
In Kamloops;
But I cannot canoe
At a quarter to two
In a van when the traffic
Jam loops.

(Canoe?)

Freddy

Here is the story
Of Freddy, my friend,
Who ran out in traffic—
And that is the end.

CALABOGIE
KAPUKASING
ESPANOLA
ATIKOKAN
MANITOULIN
MADAWASKA

Skit, Scat

Skit, scat,
Scaredy-cat:
Scoot, skedaddle
And don't come back!

Catching

The boys catch the girls
And the girls catch the boys:
Kissing in the schoolyard,
What a yucky noise!

Meet Me

Meet me at the parking lot,
Meet me in the ditch,
Meet me at the corner
With the seven year itch!

Spaghetti-o!

Oh-oh, spaghetti-o:
Eat it with confetti-o.
When it's ready, let it go!
Oh-oh, spaghetti-o:

Eh, Mon

Eh, mon,
Cool, mon—
You a silly
Fool, mon.

Double-barrelled Ding-dong-bat

Why,
You—

Double-barrelled,
Disconnected,
Supersonic
Ding-dong-bat:

Don't you dare come
Near me, or I'll
Disconnect you
Just like that!

Dirty Georgie

Georgie's face was
Never clean,
Georgie smelled like
Gasoline.

Kissing Georgie—
Mighty fine!
Just like kissing
Frankenstein!

Georgie, Georgie,
Wash your face,
Or we'll kick you out
Of the human race:

Not because you're ugly,
Not because you're cute,
Just because your dirty ears
Smell like rubber boots!

News of the Day

Neighbour, neighbour, tell me do:
What's the news at noon?

Believe it or not, an astronaut
Is walking on the moon.

Jenny Shall Ride

Jenny shall ride in a carriage,
Jenny shall ride on a sleigh.
And I'll be the king of tomorrow,
And she shall be queen of today.

33

The Maple Tree

My maple tree
Is neat to climb,
And there's a special
Branch of mine

Where I can perch
And not be seen,
And watch the world
Go by, and dream.

Shoo, Doggie, Shoo!

Shoo, doggie, shoo!
I'm not in love with you.
    You like to fight,
      And your teeth might bite,
So shoo, doggie, shoo!

Mr Lister's Dog

Mr Lister lost his dog,
And Mrs Lister found him,
And Sister Lister fetched him home
And tied a ribbon round him.

Carey Cut

Carey cut the back yard,
Carey cut the front;
Carey cut the house in two—
What a silly stunt!

Over and Over

Over and
     Over,
Come over
     To me:
I'll be your
     Friend if
You want me
     To be.

Cookies and
     Juice, at
A quarter
     To three:
Over and
     Over,
Come over
     To me.

Under the Garden Hose

Dinkelpuss, and Twinkletoes,
And Chuck-Me-Under-the-Chin,
All ran under the garden hose
To see if they could swim.

The water felt so hot,
The water felt so cold,
The water felt like soda pop
And now my tale is told.

Knock! Knock!

Knock! Knock!
    Who's there?
Captain Cook
    In his underwear.

Knock! Knock!
    Who's that?
Jacques Cartier
    In a tall silk hat.

Doctor, Doctor

Doctor, Doctor, fix my head:
I'm feeling sick and I'll soon be dead!

Little girl, little girl, drink some juice:
You think too much and your brain's come loose.

Doctor, Doctor, here's a dime:
You saved my life for the forty-second time.

Sailing to Sea

I'm sailing to sea in the bathroom,
    And I'm swimming to sea in a tub,
And the only song that I ever will sing
    Is rub-a-dub dub-a-dub dub.

A duck and a dog and a submarine
    Are sailing together with me,
And it's rub-a-dub-dub
And it's dub-a-dub-dub
    As we all sail out to sea.

The Voyage

The cowboy and the carpenter,
The collie and the cook,
Sailed the blue Pacific
On a telephone book.

They sailed for forty nights.
They sailed for forty days.
They gobbled tons of hot cross buns
With a dab of mayonnaise.

Rock Me Easy

(very slowly)

Rock me easy,
  Rock me slow,
And rock me where
  The robins go,

And rock the branch,
  And rock the bough,
And rock the baby
  Robins now,

And rock them up
  And rock them down
And rock them off
  To sleepy town,

And rock me slowly
  Up the stairs
To snuggle down
  With my teddy bears,

And rock me easy,
  Rock me slow,
And rock me where
  The robins go.

The Little Old Man

A little old man
Went up in space,
And he got ice cream
All over his face,

Sooo—

Wash him with a wash-cloth,
Roll him in a rug,
And tuck him in a blanket
Till he's snug, snug, snug!

The Bear and the Bees

Wiggle waggle went the bear,
Catching bees in his underwear.
One bee out,
And one bee in,
And one bee bit him
On his big bear skin.

The Tiny Perfect Mayor

A tiny perfect mayor
        With a tum, tum, tum,
Tried to toddle round the block
        To meet his mum, mum, mum.
He took a tiny tumble
        On a crumb, crumb, crumb,
And he cried, "I wish I'd never
        Ever come, come, come."

Bigamy Bill

Bigamy Bill,
Bigamy Bill,
Kept three wives
On a window sill.

One wife hit,
And one wife bit,
And one wife beat him
With a hickory stick.

Dopey the Dinosaur

I had a little dinosaur
And Dopey was his name.
At one o'clock he ran away,
At two o'clock he came.

At three o'clock he bothered me,
At four o'clock he stopped,
At five o'clock he fetched the leash
And took me for a walk.

43

TORONTOSAURUS REX

Torontosaurus Rex,
Torontosaurus Rex!
Tiny in the brain, but
Enormous in the neck.

Taller than the CN Tower,
Bigger than Quebec:
Don't fool around with
Torontosaurus Rex!

The Dinosaur Dinner

Allosaurus, stegosaurus,
Brontosaurus too,
All went off for dinner at the
Dinosaur zoo;

Along came the waiter, called
Tyrannosaurus Rex,
Gobbled up the table
'Cause they wouldn't pay their checks.

Anna Banana

Anna Banana, jump into the stew:
Gravy and carrots are *good* for you.
   Good for your teeth,
      And your fingernails too,
So Anna Banana, jump into the stew!

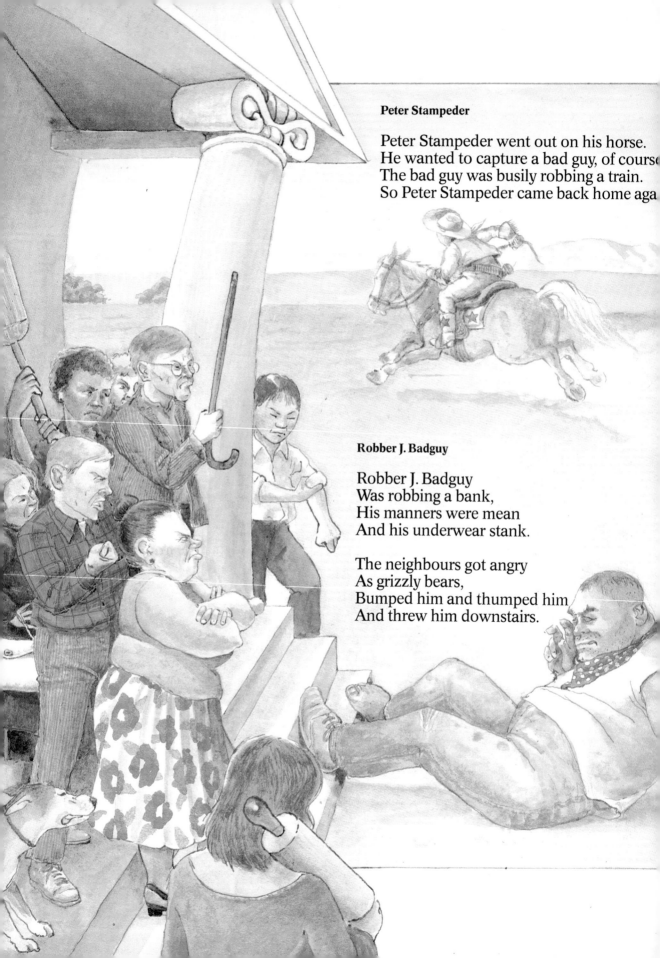

Peter Stampeder

Peter Stampeder went out on his horse.
He wanted to capture a bad guy, of course
The bad guy was busily robbing a train.
So Peter Stampeder came back home aga

Robber J. Badguy

Robber J. Badguy
Was robbing a bank,
His manners were mean
And his underwear stank.

The neighbours got angry
As grizzly bears,
Bumped him and thumped him
And threw him downstairs.

William Lyon Mackenzie

William Lyon Mackenzie
Came to town in a frenzy—
    He shot off his gun
    And made himself run,
William Lyon Mackenzie.

Peterkin Pete

Poor little Peterkin Pete:
His family had nothing to eat.
    They looked in the cupboard
    And whimpered and blubbered,
Poor little Peterkin Pete.

Brave little Peterkin Pete:
His family had nothing to eat.
    He went to the Prairies
    And picked them some berries,
Brave little Peterkin Pete!

47

The Excellent Wedding of the Broom and the Mop

Hippity, lippity, lop!
The broom shall marry the mop.
    The puppy shall bow,
    The puss shall miaow,
And the piggy shall go for the pop,
    The pop—
The piggy shall go for the pop.

Hippity, lippity, lop!
The broom has married the mop.
    The pussy got up
    For a dance with the pup,
And the piggywig guzzled the pop,
    The pop—
The piggywig guzzled the pop.

Mrs Murphy, and Mrs Murphy's Kids

Mrs Murphy,
    If you please,
Kept her kids
    In a can of peas.

The kids got bigger
    And the can filled up,
So she moved them into
    A measuring cup.

But the kids got bigger
    And the cup got crammed,
So she poured them into
    A frying pan.

But the kids grew bigger
    And the pan began to stink,
So she pitched them all
    In the kitchen sink.

But the kids kept growing
    And the sink went *kaplooey,*
So she dumped them on their ears
    In a crate of chop suey.

But the kids kept growing
    And the crate got stuck,
So she carted them away
    In a ten-ton truck.

And she said, "Thank goodness
    I remembered that truck,
Or my poor little children
    Would be out of luck!"

But the darn kids grew
　　Till the truck wouldn't fit,
And she had to haul them off
　　To a gravel pit.

But the kids kept growing
　　Till the pit was too small,
So she bedded them down
　　In a shopping mall.

But the kids grew enormous
　　And the mall wouldn't do,
So she herded them together
　　In an empty zoo.

But the kids grew gigantic
　　And the fence went *pop!*
So she towed them away
　　To a mountain top.

But the kids just grew
　　And the mountain broke apart,
And she said, "Darned kids,
　　They were pesky from the start!"

So she waited for a year,
　　And she waited for another,
And the kids grew up
　　And had babies like their mother.

And Mrs Murphy's kids—
　　You can think what you please—
Kept all *their* kids
　　In a can of peas.

My Doodle-bug Won't Come Home

My doodle-bug won't come home.
No, my doodle-bug won't come home.
   He likes to roam
   And he won't come home,
And my doodle-bug won't come home.

My doodle-bug climbed the wall.
Yes, my doodle-bug climbed the wall.
   I said he'd fall
   If he climbed a wall,
But my doodle-bug climbed the wall.

And my doodle-bug won't come home.
No, my doodle-bug won't come home.
   He likes to roam
   And he's *still* not home,
And my doodle-bug won't come home.

Pussy-willow

Pussy-willow,
     Pussy-willow,
Like a cater-
     Pillar's pillow—
Spring is near
     When you appear,
Pussy-willow
     Mine-o.

Granny Spider

Granny Spider
Sits and knits,
She sits and knits
With all her wits.
She spins a line
Of silky twine,
And sits and knits all day.

The Queen of Sheba's Daughter

The Queen of Sheba's daughter
Ran around the house,
Up and down the banister,
Frightened by a mouse.

The Queen of Sheba's daughter
Ran across the ceiling.
The mousie clapped and chased her back—
Once more, with feeling.

Little Mr Mousiekin

Little Mr Mousiekin
Sitting in your housiekin,
Eating bread and barley corn—
Little Mr Mousiekin.

Zinga, Zinga

Zinga, zinga, zumpkin:
A pussy on a pumpkin.
*A puss in the light
But a witch at night!*
Zinga, zinga, zumpkin.

The Ghost and Jenny Jemima

(slow and spooky)

The clock struck one,
The clock struck two,
The ghost came playing
Peekaboo.
    Wa-OOO!
    Wa-OOO!

The clock struck three,
The clock struck four,
And Jenny Jemima
Began to roar.
    Wa-OOO!
    Wa-OOO!

The clock struck five,
The clock struck six,
The ghost could walk through
Steel and bricks.
    Wa-OOO!
    Wa-OOO!

The clock struck seven,
The clock struck eight,
And Jenny Jemima's
Hair stood straight.
    Wa-OOO!
    Wa-OOO!

The clock struck nine,
The clock struck ten…
The ghost wound the clock,
And went home again.

THE END.

The Birthday Present

There was a little guy
With a twinkle in his eye,
And he hadn't any money
For to spend, spend, spend.

So he made a wooden flute
With a root-toot-toot,
And he played it at the party
For his friend, friend, friend.

Thumbelina

Thumbelina came to town,
Pigtails up and petticoats down,
All the children crowding round—
    Tiny Thumbelina!

Thumbelina, dance on my thumb,
Tap your toes with a rum-tum-tum!
Boys on piano, girls on drum—
    Play for Thumbelina!

Up in North Ontario

Up in North Ontario
A barber met a bear-io
And cut his curly hair-io,
Up in North Ontario.

Christmas Tree

Christmas tree,
    You're green as green,
The prettiest tree
    I've ever seen,

The shiniest tree
    I've ever known—
I'll dream about you
    When I'm grown.

The Snowstorm

Heave-ho,
Buckets of snow,
The giant is combing his beard.
The snow is as high
As the top of the sky,
And the world has disappeared.

Going, Going, Gone

Going, going, gone,
Your daddy won't be long.
Where did he go?
To shovel the snow.
Going, going, gone.

The Gentle Giant

Every night
At twelve o'clock,
The gentle giant
Takes a walk;
With a cry cried high
And a call called low,
The gentle giant
Walks below.

And as he walks,
He cries, he calls:

*"Bad men, boogie men,
Bully men, shoo!
No one in the neighbourhood
Is scared of you.
The children are asleep,
And the parents are too:
Bad men, boogie men,
Bully men, shoo!"*

Good Night, Good Night

The dark is dreaming.
   Day is done.
Good night, good night
   To everyone.

Good night to the birds,
   And the fish in the sea,
Good night to the bears
   And good night to me.

Silverly

Silverly,
  Silverly,
Over the
  Trees
The moon drifts
  By on a
Runaway
  Breeze.

Dozily,
  Dozily,
Deep in her
  Bed,
A little girl
  Dreams with the
Moon in her
  Head.